MW01124200

Christmas

ABC

Janet Warren Herbert ♥

D **Deer** are taking flight

E

ELves
are in a tizzy

H Hot chocolate
and cider
for you and for me

Kids
are
what it is all about...

...without a doubt!

L

Lights
in every color
and shape

O Ornaments are unpacked with Special Care

P

Parades and Parties are really fun

S

SANTA
NEVER Goes
to bed

·Santa·

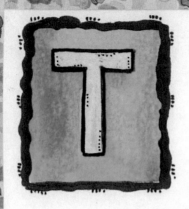

T

Trees
are TALL and
and beautiful
and BRIGHT

Unwrapping
can Leave a Mess in sight

Wreaths
seem to
Last and Last

Christmas

Xmas and **XOXOXO** is what it is ALL About... ...without a DOUBT

 XMAS

Yummy
food and candy
is always sitting out

Z

Zzzzs
and
Zzzzzs

are coming

and
when it is all done...

Hoping and Dreaming
About
next Christmas to come

and
to all
a
Goodnight

A B C Christmas

LEARNING

the

ALPHABET

is a

FOUNDATIONAL

SKILL for

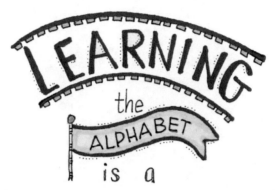

READING WRITING AND

COMMUNICATING

The Alphabet is a

stepping STONE and a

MILESTONE

INTO a WORLD of

★ Endless Possibilities ★

Janet Warren Herbert is the owner of Happy Things, an art business started forty-six years ago specializing in gifts. She has a B.S. in English and Physical Sciences and lives in Vail, Colorado after moving from the panhandle of Texas. She is the illustrator for twenty books. Her joyful art is inspired by her love for her husband and four children and nine grandchildren.

Draw
your favorite gift or memory

my
Christmas
LIST

1 _____

2 _____

3 _____

4 _____

5 _____

Made in the USA
Middletown, DE
10 September 2022

73510046R00020